THE
LORD'S
PRAYER

How Jesus Taught Us to
Talk to Our Father

TERRY MYERS

WESTBOW
PRESS®
A DIVISION OF THOMAS NELSON
& ZONDERVAN

WestBow Press books may be ordered through booksellers or by contacting:

WestBow Press
A Division of Thomas Nelson & Zondervan
1663 Liberty Drive
Bloomington, IN 47403
www.westbowpress.com
844-714-3454

Unless marked otherwise, all Scripture quotations are taken from The Holy Bible, New International Version®, NIV® Copyright © 1973, 1978, 1984, 2011 by Biblica, Inc.® Used by permission. All rights reserved worldwide.

Scripture quotations marked NLT are taken from the Holy Bible, New Living Translation, Copyright © 1996, 2004, 2015 by Tyndale House Foundation. Used by permission of Tyndale House Publishers, Inc., Carol Stream, Illinois 60188. All rights reserved.

Scripture quotations marked KJV are taken from the King James Version.

Scripture quotations marked ESV taken from The Holy Bible, English Standard Version® (ESV®), Copyright © 2001 by Crossway, a publishing ministry of Good News Publishers. All rights reserved.

ISBN: 978-1-6642-0436-2 (sc)
ISBN: 978-1-6642-0438-6 (hc)
ISBN: 978-1-6642-0437-9 (e)

Library of Congress Control Number: 2020916874

Print information available on the last page.

WestBow Press rev. date: 11/19/2020

Contents

Acknowledgements

To my home group:
Thank you for encouraging me,
and even pushing me,
to step out and publish
this book.
Thank you.

To my four children:
Robert, Jennifer, Vicki and Christina.
I love you more than words
can say,
and I am so proud of you.

"Children are a gift from the LORD."
(Psalm 27:3)

All your children will be
taught by the Lord,
and great will be
your children's peace.
(Isaiah 54:13)

Introduction

When I was little, I learned that prayer was talking to God. That was all well and good, I thought, but what was I supposed to say to Him? And since God was bigger and smarter than me, I thought I'd better do it correctly.

It seemed to me that prayer was mostly for saying thank you and asking for stuff, whatever I needed. In the church I grew up in, we had special prayers for everything written by people much more knowledgeable and definitely holier than I was, but I had trouble connecting with those prayers. I felt I was just reading words; I thought that if I could just pray the right way, I'd get answers.

So my prayer life has been a journey for over forty years. I've learned to worship, to pray scripture, to intercede for others, to give thanks, to pray specifically, and to not be specific but trust God's will in situations, but still, it didn't seem quite complete.

Several years ago, I asked the Lord for a word at the beginning of the year, and I heard the word *prayer* in my mind. The disciples asked Jesus to teach them to pray. Who could be a more perfect teacher! His response is what we now know as The Lord's Prayer.

I started looking for books about the Lord's Prayer. That inner voice said, *You write one.* Really? I told the Lord several times that I wasn't a writer, but He didn't listen, so I wrote this book.

It contains what I believe the Lord has shown me about this prayer. It's not a theological document, and it doesn't contain all the truth on this subject, but it's how praying as Jesus taught has blessed me and deepened my relationship with Father God.

I hope it blesses you too.

What about Prayer?

Our Father who art in Heaven,

Hallowed be Thy name.

Thy Kingdom come.

Thy will be done

On earth, as it is in Heaven.

Give us this day our daily bread.

And forgive us our debts,

As we forgive our debtors.

And lead us not into temptation,

But deliver us from evil.

Amen.

—Matthew 6:9–13

I learned the Our Father in school when I was young. It was the prayer Jesus taught His disciples to pray, and if it was good enough for them, it was good enough for me.

Occasionally, I'd think about the meaning, but back then, it was just a memorized prayer.

Later, after choosing to follow Jesus, I started paying more attention to the words and especially the "forgive me as I forgive others" part. But there is so much more here. What was Jesus really trying to tell His followers?

Jesus began His public ministry and called twelve men to follow him. These were not the cream of society but ordinary people just like you and me. Follow Jesus they did; they listened to His teachings and watched Him perform miracles, and then Jesus sent them out to do the same things! But Jesus had this way of getting away by Himself no matter who needed what, no matter how tired He was, and no matter where He was. They must have seen how this affected Jesus because they wanted what He had. And they wanted to know how to pray as he prayed.

What Is Prayer?

Merriam-Webster's defines prayer as making a request in a humble manner, addressing God or a god with adoration, confession, supplication, or thanksgiving. So prayer is basically talking to God in worship, confession, praise, thanksgiving, or petition. Talking to God? That seems pretty simple, but …

When's the Best Time of Day to Pray?

According to Mark 1:35, the best time to pray is early: "Very early in the morning, while it was still dark, Jesus got up, left the house and went off to a solitary place, where he prayed." But in Luke 6:12 (NLT), we read, "Jesus went up on a mountain to pray, and he prayed to God all night." So, Jesus also prayed at night.

I've spent a lot of years beating myself up for not getting up really early to spend time in prayer; I wasn't a morning person. What I've learned is that it doesn't matter when we pray; what matters is that we do pray. In 1 Thessalonians 5:16–18 (ESV), we read, "Rejoice always; pray without ceasing, give thanks in all circumstances; for this is the will of God in Christ Jesus for you." So there is never a time not to pray.

Where Should We Pray?

According to Luke 5:16, "Jesus often withdrew to lonely places and prayed." Mark 1:35 says, "Jesus got up, left the house and went off to a solitary place, where he prayed."

Getting alone time with God has been a challenge for me.

It seems that as soon as I pull away to pray, everyone starts looking for me. Or I fall asleep.

Matthew 6:6 tells us, "When you pray, go into your room, close the door and pray to your Father who is unseen. Then your Father who sees what is done in secret, will reward you." Sometimes, that's easier said than done. In the movie *War Room*, the characters actually converted a closet into a prayer room. That works if you have an extra closet, but you can possibly go to your bedroom and close the door, take a walk alone, sit in your car during lunch, or turn off the TV and sit in your favorite chair. Find out what works for you. If you have little ones, you may need to be more creative.

Susanna Wesley (mother of ten, including Charles and John) had no place to be by herself, but she had promised to give God two hours a day. She told her children that when her apron was over her head, she was not to be bothered; that was her God time. I personally cannot imagine my kids being quiet enough for that or not bothering me, but she made it work for her.

Why Should I Pray?

Jesus had an unending fellowship within the Trinity even when He was on earth. Yes, He had disciples, but that didn't compare to his spending time with His Father. Prayer is an act of communion with God; it's not just talking for the sake of talking or reciting a laundry list of requests. It is spending time with our heavenly Father, who loves us and delights in us, His children.

Have you ever had "communion" with friends who used very colorful language or had a rough manner? Soon, you started using the same words, picking up the same attitudes, and so on. When we spend time with our heavenly Father, His character starts to rub off on us. Our talk changes, our attitudes change, our likes and dislikes change, and so on. We start to really know Him as He knows us. We start to resemble our Father.

What Should I Say in Prayer?

Psalm 100:4 says, "Enter His gates with thanksgiving, and His courts with praise!" This is a great place to start. We have so much to be thankful for, and He more than deserves praise and worship. This also helps us get our minds off our "light and momentary troubles" and onto Him. (2 Corinthians 4:17) Acknowledge His greatness, goodness, and holiness.

Give Him thanks for all blessings and for what He's doing with stuff we don't yet see as blessings.

Romans 8:26–28 (NLT) reads,

And the Holy Spirit helps us in our weakness. For example, we don't know what God wants us to pray for. *But the Holy Spirit prays for us* with groanings that cannot be expressed in words. And the Father who knows all hearts knows what the Spirit is saying, for the Spirit pleads for us believers in harmony with God's own will. And we know that God causes everything to work together for the good of those who love God and are called according to his purpose for them. (emphasis mine)

We are all familiar with the phrase "all things work together for good"; it comes from this passage. But look at the context here. When we pray, when we ask the Holy Spirit to help us pray, when we pray in line with God's will, when we give the situation to God, that's when all things work together for good; that's when God turns our tests into our testimony.

Romans 8:31–34 (NLT) asks,

What shall we say about such wonderful things as these? If God is for us, who can ever be against us? Since he did not spare even his own Son but gave him up for us all, won't he also give us everything else? Who dares accuse us whom God has chosen for his own? No one— for God himself has given us right standing with himself. Who then will condemn us? No one—for Christ Jesus died for us and was raised to life for us, and he is sitting in the place of honor at God's right hand, pleading for us.

Hebrews 4:16 (NLT) reads,

So, let us come *boldly* to the *throne* of our gracious God. There, we will receive his mercy, and we will find grace to help us when we need it most. (emphasis mine)

Because of what Jesus did on the cross, God is not mad at us; we are not under condemnation. We can go to him confidently and boldly.

Have you ever wondered what Jesus and the Holy Spirit are praying? One thing they are not doing is complaining about the situations you are in or stressing about all the junk going on and wondering what to do about it. They are agreeing with one another and Father God about you—how much they love you, what they have promised to do for you, what blessings they have for you, what they want you to learn about next, and so on.

So when we pray, it's a good idea to agree with what God says. Yes, we can tell Him our needs. He knows them already, but He says to bring our petitions and needs to Him. But it's also important to agree with Him and thank Him for His promises, faithfulness, goodness, provision, healing, and the other blessings He gives us. We may not see the whole picture, but that doesn't change the fact that He is good and loving and always keeps His promises.

> **God is good all the time; and**
> **all the time, God is good.**

How Should I Pray?

Jesus said, "When you pray, say …" (Luke 11:2). So often, I have been praying in my head and the next thing I know, my mind has wandered to who knows where, usually meditating on a problem, my fears, my busyness. So say what you pray aloud whenever you can; that releases power into the atmosphere against the "the devil—the commander of the powers in the unseen world" (Ephesians 2:2 NLT). This can be at whatever volume you like. You can pray quietly, under your breath. You can sing to Him. You can even scream at God; He can take it. You can scream at the enemy too; volume won't faze him, but speaking God's Word will! And don't stop there; continue with thanking God and praising Him for who He is. Continue declaring what God says is true; that's so important. Many of the psalms start with David telling God what was wrong and that it looked like God was doing nothing about it! And then, David would use one of my favorite Bible phrases, "But God …" Yes, God, this is wrong, and that is wrong, and my enemies are doing stuff, but God, you are holy and good, and I will trust you!

Would you like it if your kids talked to you only when they wanted something? Or if they had a relationship with you based solely on what you did or didn't do for them? Would you like it if they didn't share their hopes, dreams, and problems with you? Well, God wants conversation with us too. He cares about every aspect of our lives. Nothing is too big or too small for Him. Even when we're in a rotten situation, we can thank and praise God for who He is even if we don't like what it looks like He is doing or not doing. And don't forget to thank Him for the everyday things such as waking up, food, freedom, health, work, family, the beauty of nature—the list of what you can thank Him for goes on and on.

Another option we have is to write out our prayers, which is also a good way to learn to hear the Lord. I've found that it slows down and unjumbles my thoughts. I'm less like Ricochet Rabbit and more focused when I write down my prayers. Years ago, I was complaining to a friend that I couldn't hear God. She asked, "What's the first thing that pops into your mind after you ask God something?" All I could say was, "Who knows? My thoughts don't take numbers!"

After writing down your prayers and what you are thankful for, just listen. Good conversations are two-way matters. Write down the thoughts going through your mind or the feelings you're experiencing; that will help you learn to hear God's voice. These thoughts sound like your voice, your thoughts, but the content behind those thoughts—the love, the attitude, the goodness, the hope, the peace—is coming from beyond you. It may be only a few words or the feeling that God is happy to be spending time with you, or that He loves you or whomever you are praying for, or something else. You may think of a friend to call. He may give you an idea that you know is too good to be yours. These are so precious. I often go back and read my journal entries. Love it!

Discussion Questions

Do you ever feel the need to withdraw? What do you do? Where do you go?

Do you pray quietly? In your head? Out loud?

Does your mind wander in prayer? Do you ever run out of words?

Do you journal?

Do you pray about the little stuff that's bothering you?

Are you aware of any answered prayers?

Prayer

Jesus, as you did with your disciples, I ask that you teach me to pray. If you needed to pray, I certainly do.

Holy Spirit, I really need your help here. I don't always know what to pray, and I even have trouble remembering to pray. Please help me find my quiet place and my quiet time. Help me to "be still and know that You are God." (Psalm 46:10) You have said that you are my helper, so I'm counting on your help.

I thank you for all the help you are giving me and will give me.

Oh, and Lord, please help me learn to recognize your voice just as lambs know their shepherd's voice. Thank you.

Amen.

Our Father, Who Art in Heaven

When the disciples asked Jesus to teach them how to pray, Jesus started with these words. Why? Why did Jesus specify our Father "in heaven"? Isn't the "in heaven" rather obvious?

I believe He specified this because there are two fathers, God and Satan. Surprised? Look at what Jesus said to the Jewish leaders in John 8:38–44.

> "I am telling you what I have seen in the Father's presence, and you are doing what you have heard from your father." "Abraham is our father," they answered. "If you were Abraham's children," said Jesus, "then you would do what Abraham did. As it is, you are looking for a way to kill me, a man who has told you the truth that I heard from God. Abraham did not do such things. You are doing the works of your

own father." "We are not illegitimate children," they protested. "The only Father we have is God himself."

Jesus said to them, "If God were your Father, you would love me, for I have come here from God. I have not come on my own; God sent me.

Why is my language not clear to you? Because you are unable to hear what I say. You belong to your father, the devil, and you want to carry out your father's desires. He was a murderer from the beginning, not holding to the truth, for there is no truth in him. When he lies, he speaks his native language, for he is a liar and the father of lies."

Jesus was talking about two fathers—Satan and His Father. I've heard people argue that everyone is a child of God, that everyone has God as his or her Father. This is God's heart—why we were created—but since the fall of Adam and Eve, everyone automatically being a child of God is just not true or Jesus would not have said that Satan was their father.

It is impossible to be a child of the devil and a child of God at the same time. That's why we need to be born again.

Why did Jesus tell the disciples to call God "Father"? Why not some other name or title? Did anyone pray to God as Father in the Old Testament? Not really. In the Old Testament, God introduced Himself as Father in how He cared for His people. For example, Psalm 27:10 (NLT) reads, "Even if my father and mother abandon me, the LORD will hold me close." However, it was usually more in context as the Father of His people, not necessarily personally to each of His people.

> But you are our Father, though Abraham does not know us or Israel acknowledge us; you, O LORD, are our Father, our Redeemer from of old is your name. (Isaiah 63:16)

> When Israel was a child, I loved him, and out of Egypt I called my son. But the more they were called, the more they went away from me. They sacrificed to the Baals and they burned incense to images. It was I who taught Ephraim to walk, taking them by the arms; but they did

not realize it was I who healed them. I led them with cords of human kindness, with ties of love. To them I was like one who lifts a little child to the cheek, and I bent down to feed them. (Hosea 11:1– 4)

Although God loved them as a Father, they didn't really understand, and Jesus hadn't yet made the way to the Father. Jesus came to show us His Father and to lead us to Him.

Philip said, "Lord, show us the Father and that will be enough for us." Jesus answered: "Don't you know me, Philip, even after I have been among you such a long time? Anyone who has seen me has seen the Father. How can you say, 'Show us the Father'? Don't you believe that I am in the Father, and that the Father is in me? The words I say to you I do not speak on my own authority. Rather, it is the Father, living in me, who is doing his work. Believe me when I say that I am in the Father and the Father is in me; or at least believe on the evidence of the works themselves." (John 14:8–11)

Jesus said to them, "My Father is always at his work to this very day, and I, too, am working." For this reason, the Jews tried all the harder to kill him; not only was he breaking the Sabbath, but he was even calling God his own Father, making himself equal with God. (John 5:17–18)

Jesus was in trouble with the leaders and was almost stoned because He called God His Father. One time, they tried to throw Him off a cliff! To the Jews, Jesus was claiming too close of a relationship with God. However, He told us to pray from that same position—that of a Father and much-loved child. He could have taught us to pray, "O most powerful potentate. We bow in fear before you. How can we serve you? How can we satisfy your great anger towards us? How can we make you pleased with us?" Other people prayed to their gods that way. But no, He said to pray, "Our Father." That is His heart's desire.

Many of us have trouble relating to God as Father. Maybe we didn't have a father in our lives, or we wished he wasn't in our lives because he was anything but godlike. In any event, our fathers were human with faults, so our picture of what a father is supposed to be like may be somewhat tarnished.

What does the word *father* means to you? Here are some questions to ask yourself.

- Was your dad affectionate or distant?
- Was he often or always angry?
- Was your dad happy to see you?
- Was he glad to be your dad?
- Was he proud of you?
- Did you feel you had to do the right thing for him to be pleased with you?
- Did he have time for you?
- Did you feel you belonged?
- Did your dad help you discover who you are? Do you know who you are?
- Could you talk to him? Could you talk about your dreams, fears, hurts, relationships, and so on?
- What did you inherit from your father? Good stuff? Bad stuff? (Most likely both!)

Here are a few scriptures that tell us about God the Father and how He loves us.

Praise the Lord, my soul; all my inmost being, praise his holy name.

Praise the Lord, my soul, and forget not all his benefits—

who forgives all your sins and heals all your diseases,

who redeems your life from the pit and crowns you with love and compassion,

who satisfies your desires with good things so that your youth is renewed like the eagle's.

The Lord works righteousness and justice for all the oppressed.

He made known his ways to Moses, his deeds to the people of Israel:

The Lord is compassionate and gracious, slow to anger, abounding in love.

He will not always accuse, nor will he harbor his anger forever;

he does not treat us as our sins deserve or repay us according to our iniquities.

For as high as the heavens are above the earth, so great is his love for those who fear him;

as far as the east is from the west, so far has he removed our transgressions from us.

As a father has compassion on his children, so the Lord has compassion on those who fear him; (Psalm 103:1–13; emphasis mine. The whole psalm is wonderful!)

All praise to God, the Father of our Lord Jesus Christ, who has blessed us with every spiritual blessing in the heavenly realms because we are united with Christ. Even before he made the world, God *loved us* and *chose us* in Christ to be holy and without fault in his eyes. God decided in advance *to adopt us into his own family* by bringing us to himself through Jesus Christ. This is what he wanted to do, and it gave him great pleasure. So we praise God for the glorious grace he has poured out on us who belong to his dear Son. He is so rich in kindness and grace that he purchased our freedom with the blood of his Son and forgave our sins. He has showered his kindness on us, along with all wisdom and understanding.

And now you Gentiles have also heard the truth, the Good News that God saves you. *And when you believed in Christ, he identified you as his own* by giving you the Holy Spirit, whom he promised long ago. The Spirit is God's guarantee that he will give us the inheritance he promised and that he has purchased us to be his own people. He did this so we would praise and glorify him. (Ephesians 1:3–8, 13–14 NLT; emphasis mine)

God chose us before the foundation of the world! He knew we would need saving, and He decided in advance to pay the price. He wanted us to be His children, and we give him great pleasure. We get our identity from our fathers. We are who our heavenly Father says we are, and we get an inheritance!

The eyes of the Lord are on the righteous and his ears are attentive to their cry; but the face of the Lord is against those who do evil, to blot out their name from the earth. The righteous cry out, and the Lord hears them; he delivers them from all their troubles. (Psalm 34:15–17)

Discussion Questions

What does the word *father* mean to you?

What was your father like? Was he a daddy? A disciplinarian?

Was he distant emotionally or gone a lot?

Could you crawl into his lap? Could you really talk to him?

How do you feel about God being your Father? Is that a safe thought, a happy thought, or you don't really relate to God as Father at all?

What did you call your father? Can you imagine calling God Daddy or Papa, or Abba?

Prayer

> Jesus, you had such a close relationship with your Father when you were here on earth. I want to be closer to Father God too. I thank you for my earthly father even though he wasn't perfect.

I choose to forgive my earthly father for any ways he failed me when I was growing up. At times, he said or did things that hurt me very much. There were times that I needed him but he wasn't there. I place all those times and hurts in your loving hands. And if I remember any more, I'll give them to you too. Please bless my dad. Also, please forgive me for the times I wasn't a perfect child.

Father God, thank you that because of what Jesus did for me, I am adopted into your family. I am your child, and you aren't angry with me. Thank you for always hearing me, for your love and compassion. Thank you that you know who you have created me to be.

Because of you, I belong. Help me see myself through your eyes. Thank you for not becoming frustrated with me and for knowing me completely, loving me anyway, and never giving up on me.

Thank you for satisfying my desires with good things—what you know is good for me and when. Thank you for wanting to spend time with me. Help me draw closer to you, amen.

Hallowed Be Thy Name

On first glance, this section of the Lord's Prayer seems to be just a reminder to not cuss using God's name. We are told in Exodus 20:7, "You shall not misuse the name of the Lord your God, for the Lord will not hold anyone guiltless who misuses his name." This is a reminder to us to not misuse God's name, but I believe there is much more to pray here.

God wants a relationship with us. He knows us completely, and He wants us to know Him, not just know about Him. I believe we can never know everything about Him—He's just that big—but He continually wants to reveal Himself to us. All through the Old Testament, God revealed aspects of Himself to His people, and when He did, people would call Him by a new name or name the place according to how they had come to know Him.

We are not talking about names of other gods, those that

aren't the one, true God. Many people believe that all gods are the same with just different names; God is god, so to speak. Allah is god. Buddha is god. Krishna is god. Actually, India has millions of gods. These are not just other names for God; they are not all the same.

For one thing, the only one who died and rose again is Jesus. The others are all still dead. The way they relate to their followers and their personalities are different—no comparison. Allah, Buddha, and so on are not just other names for God.

Let's get to know our God and heavenly Father better.

Yahweh: I Am

In Exodus, God called Moses to go back to Egypt and rescue His people living in slavery. When Moses had left Egypt, he'd been running for his life.

We read in Exodus 3:13–15,

Moses said to God, "Suppose I go to the Israelites and say to them, 'The God of your fathers has sent me to you,' and they ask me, 'What is his name?' Then what shall I tell them?" God said to, Moses, "**I am who I am.** This is what you are to say to the Israelites: 'I am has sent me to you.'" God also said to Moses, "Say to the Israelites, 'The Lord, the God of your fathers— the God of Abraham, the God of Isaac and the God of Jacob—has sent me to you.'"

This has been hard for me to wrap my brain around. If I were standing at the burning bush, I'd be asking, "I Am? You're what?" Jesus tells us some of what this means in the gospel of John, and here are a few of them. It is interesting that He didn't introduce Himself as just God. No. He said, "I am who I am" (Exodus 3:14).

- I am the Bread of Life (John 6:35)
- I am the Light of the World (John 8:12)
- I am the Good Shepherd (John 10:11)
- I am the Resurrection and the Life (John 11:25)
- I am the Way, the Truth, and the Life (John 14:6)
- I am the vine and you are the branches (John 15:5)

Our God always was, is now, and always will be whatever we need—and more.

El Shaddai—God Almighty—All-Sufficient God

When Abram was ninety-nine, the Lord appeared to him and said, "I am God Almighty; walk before me faithfully and be blameless" (Genesis 17:1).

This is one of God's names that became very special to me. In Hebrew, this is El Shaddai—God almighty, God all-powerful. No one and nothing are more powerful than our God. With so much not good happening in the world today, I'm glad we have a big God.

Some ask, "If God is so powerful, why doesn't He stop all the bad things happening in the world?" Books have been written on this subject. A short answer is that sin, sickness, and death were not here when God created this world. When God gave us free will, He wasn't kidding. He doesn't take His gifts back just because we misuse them even though He is powerful enough to do so. Starting with Adam and Eve, humankind has made some bad choices. Satan gained authority on earth and has used that to wreak all kinds of havoc. We'll talk more about this in an upcoming lesson.

Here is another more hidden meaning in this name of God. It was once explained to me that a root meaning of this is "many breasted." So strange. I actually looked it up. Now that can evoke a strange picture in our minds, but I'd like to suggest another aspect. Picture a female dog that delivers nine puppies - with only eight places to nurse. One of them is going to have trouble getting enough! Coming from a very large family, I never really felt there was enough mom to go around or enough of anything else at times. Remember that movie *Bruce Almighty* with Jim Carrey? He was overloaded and overwhelmed by all the prayers of all the people! El Shaddai is not like that. He is sufficient. His resources are endless. His love is boundless. And He is never too busy to listen or help. He can handle my, your, and everyone else's needs too. He is always enough!

El Elyon—Most High God

> But Abram said to the king of Sodom, "With raised hand I have sworn an oath to the LORD, God Most High, Creator of heaven and earth." (Genesis 14:22)

I cry out to God Most High, to God, who
vindicates me. (Psalm 57:2)

There is so much going on in the world; it can be very
scary. Terrorism. Financial problems. War. Cancer. Sickness.
Talk about the end of the world. Politics. Yuck! Too much! I
have no solutions to these problems, and I don't know anyone
who does. I am very comforted to know that God is higher
than all these problems, higher than all our enemies. He can
handle it all.

Jehovah Jireh—The Lord Will Provide

In Genesis 22, we read that God tested Abraham. God
had revealed himself to Abraham and made promises to him.
They had a blood covenant, a contract that could be broken
only by death. God would give him a son through whom all
the nations would be blessed. When God made this promise,
Abraham was ninety-nine and Sarah was ninety, and they had
to wait for Isaac to be born. Can you imagine being pregnant
at age ninety let alone chasing a two-year-old?

Then God tested Abraham; he told him to offer Isaac as a
sacrifice. I cannot imagine what that did to Abraham. He'd

waited so long for a son. What had he gotten himself into with this covenant? And all God's promises to him were tied to this son. Was the Lord trying to back out of His promises? He believed God, but he wondered how this was supposed to work. It made no sense to him. Was the Lord just toying with him?

> After these things God tested Abraham and said to him, "Abraham!" And he said, "Here am I." He said, "Take your son, your only son Isaac, whom you love, and go to the land of Moriah, and offer him there as a burnt offering on one of the mountains of which I shall tell you." (Genesis 22:1–2 ESV)

Abraham obeyed. I've always wondered if Sarah even knew or what she did or said about this. I certainly wouldn't have been silent! She too had waited a long time for that child. Abraham obeyed even though his heart was breaking. But God … I love those words. But God knew that this act of obedience would mean that God would now have to offer His only son. That is how blood covenants work. And God also knew that he would provide the lamb for the sacrifice for

Abraham and for us. But Abraham didn't know that; he just trusted and obeyed.

> But the angel of the Lord called to him from heaven and said, "Abraham, Abraham!" And he said, "Here I am." He said, "Do not lay your hand on the boy or do anything to him, for now I know that you fear God, seeing you have not withheld your son, your only son, from me." And Abraham lifted up his eyes and looked, and behold, behind him was a ram, caught in a thicket by his horns. And Abraham went and took the ram and offered it up as a burnt offering instead of his son. So, Abraham called the name of that place, "The Lord will provide"; as it is said to this day, "On the mount of the Lord it shall be provided." And the angel of the Lord called to Abraham a second time from heaven and said, "By myself I have sworn, declares the LORD, because you have done this and have not withheld your son, your only son, I will surely bless you." (Genesis 22:11–17 ESV)

God has provided Jesus, His Lamb, as the sacrifice for our sins. Here's a question. Is God done being our provider? I don't believe so. We are told in Hebrews 13:8 that "Jesus Christ is the same yesterday, today, and forever." He doesn't change. He is still our provider. Not our jobs. Not our talents. Not our efforts. Not the government. The Lord. Jehovah Jireh!

Emmanuel—God with Us

> The Lord himself will give you the sign. Look! The virgin will conceive a child! She will give birth to a son and will call him Immanuel (which means "God is with us"). (Isaiah 7:14 NLT)

> Be strong and courageous. Do not be afraid or terrified because of them, for the LORD your God goes with you; he will never leave you nor forsake you. (Deuteronomy 31:6)

We cannot get to God. He came to us. And not just once. He dwells with us everywhere, every day, all the time through his Holy Spirit. And He has promised to never leave us or forsake us (to give up on us, wash His hands of us, think we are too much trouble or not worth it!).

Do you feel God's presence? Yes? No? Sometimes? God's promises don't depend on our feelings. Feelings can be wonderful, but they aren't reliable indicators of what is true. God is faithful to all His promises. He is with us always whether we feel Him or not.

Jehovah-Rapha—The Lord Who Heals

God doesn't make us sick. He wants to heal, just like He wants to forgive.

> He forgives all my sins and heals all my diseases.
> (Psalm 103:3 NLT)

> He said, "If you listen carefully to the LORD your God and do what is right in his eyes, if you pay attention to his commands and keep all his decrees, I will not bring on you any of the diseases I brought on the Egyptians, for I am the LORD, who heals you." (Exodus 15:26)

So does this mean that if you get sick, you must have

sinned somehow? Isaiah 53 foretold what Jesus accomplished on the cross.

> But he was pierced for our transgressions; he was crushed for our iniquities;
>
> upon him was the chastisement that brought us peace, and with his wounds [stripes] we are healed. All we like sheep have gone astray; we have turned—every one—to his own way; and the Lord has laid on him the iniquity of us all. (Isaiah 53:5–6)

Jesus took the punishment for our sins. All of them. That's why He died on the cross. But why was He whipped? Wasn't crucifixion enough? He was scourged for our healing! He paid the penalty for our sins so we could have God as our Father, but that was only part of why He died. He also wanted us whole—healed spiritually, emotionally, and physically.

Jehovah Shammah—God Is There

> The distance around the entire city will be 6 miles. And from that day the name of the city will be "The Lord is There." (Ezekiel 48:35 NLT)

God is there. Where exactly is there? Yes, He's in heaven, but how is that supposed to help me here? Often, I pray for some people who are nowhere near me, maybe on the other side of the world or across the country. My heart will ache for them wishing I could just give them a hug or help in some way, but I can't. And even if I were there, how could I really help them? But God can. He's there!

Jehovah Shammah is there in terms of time as well as place. None of us knows what's going to happen, what we will have to face. We do know we'll win in the end because we've read the end of the Bible, but the future is intimidating. So much can happen—good and bad. What will we do? Will we be okay? Will our loved ones be okay?

God sees our future. He knows where He is leading us. He knows what we need to learn to handle what's coming. He is the Alpha and the Omega, the beginning and the end and everything in the middle too. He is Emmanuel, God with us, and He is in our future too.

Another great truth in scripture—He has good plans for all of us. He can be trusted.

> "For I know the plans I have for you," declares the LORD, "plans to prosper you and not to harm you, plans to give you hope and a future." (Jeremiah 29:11)

I do not know what the future holds, but I know Who holds the future.

Holy Is His Name—His Name Is Holy

I almost missed this name—Hallowed (holy) is His name. But what exactly is holy? Most definitions of this word include the words *sacred* and *set apart*. *Merriam-Webster's* defines holy as "exalted or worthy of complete devotion as one perfect in goodness and righteousness." Patheos.com defines holy as follows.

The Hebrew word for holy is "qodesh" and means "apartness, set-apartness, separateness, sacredness" and I would add that it should also be "otherness, transcendent and totally other" because God is totally above His creation and His creatures, including us. Holy has the idea of heaviness or weight of glory. In the New Testament, the word for holy is "hagios" and means set apart, reverend, sacred, and worthy of veneration. This word applies to God because God Himself is totally other, separate, sacred, transcendent, reverend, and set apart from every created thing.

God is totally above His creation and His creatures. I think that's a reason it's hard to wrap our heads around this idea. He is so different from us. When something is repeated in Hebrew, it speaks of importance. Repeating something three times really emphasizes the point. We are told that the angels around the throne of God continually cry out "Holy! Holy! Holy!"

Each of the four living creatures had six wings and was covered with eyes all around, even under its wings. Day and night, they never stop saying: "Holy, holy, holy is the Lord God Almighty, who was, and is, and is to come." (Revelation 4:8)

He is holy, set apart, worthy of veneration and worship. He is good. He is pure, not contaminated with anything that is not good.

This is the message we have heard from him and declare to you: God is light; in him there is no darkness at all. (1 John 1:5)

Later, John told us that God is love. His holiness and purity mean that His love is never contaminated with anything less than perfect love. He never has ulterior motives. He never does not love us, or to avoid the double negative, He always loves us. Even when we mess up! He never toys with us. He never does anything to harm us. His motive, His purpose is always love. In 1 John 4:8, we read, "Whoever does not love does not know God, because God is love."

I've listed only some of the names of God in scripture. You might wonder why He has so many names. We have all been called names that were meant to describe us—some nice, some not so nice—but we don't have anywhere near the number of names or nicknames that God does! Each of the names of God gives us a glimpse into His character, and because He is good, all of them are good. It is like looking at a beautiful diamond, each facet reflecting light, the glory of the stone. Every name of God is like another facet of who He is—His character reflecting His glory. For all eternity, we will forever be discovering more and more of our God.

Discussion Questions

Do you have trouble using God's name in an unholy manner?

Which one of these names is the most comforting to you?

Which name of God is new to you?

Which character trait of God do you have the most trouble believing?

In your current situation, how does God want to reveal Himself to you?

Prayer

> Father God, you *so* want us to know you—who you are and what you are like. You are so much more than the big guy in the sky or my higher power. You know us intimately, and you want us to know you intimately. But you, Lord, are so big, so great!

> Holy Spirit, as I think about your names, please knit my heart to yours. Help me to really know you as God, Savior, friend, lover, Lord (boss), helper, counselor, and so much more.

> When I'm alone, you are with me. And you have my back!

> When I need guidance, you are my shepherd guiding, protecting, and speaking to me.

When I can't see down the road, you will light the way, guide my steps, go before me, and you are already there.

You are my provider, and when I am in need, you are enough! Your supply is unlimited. You own the "cattle on a thousand hills," and if you can take care of the lilies of the fields and the sparrows, you can take care of me.

When I feel I don't belong, I do because you, Father, have known me and loved me since before the foundation of the world, and you have put me where and when you want me.

I can choose you because you first chose me. I am not an accident. I belong to you!

Thy Kingdom Come, Thy Will Be Done, on Earth as It Is in Heaven

The word *kingdom* comes from two words, *king* and *dominion* or *domain*. We know that a king is a ruler of a country or a territory. Per vocabulary.com, dominion is the power to rule; control of a country, region, etc. It can also refer to the land that a ruler or government controls.

In the beginning …

So God created mankind in his own image, in the image of God he created them; male and female he created them. God blessed them and said to them, Be fruitful and increase in number; fill the earth and *subdue it. Rule* over the fish in the sea and the birds in the sky and over every living creature that moves on the ground. (Genesis 1:27–28; emphasis mine)

When God created us, He gave us dominion over the earth and every living creature. That was His perfect plan from the beginning. What happened?

The LORD God took the man and put him in the Garden of Eden to work it and take care of it. And the LORD God commanded the man, "You are free to eat from any tree in the garden; but you must not eat from the tree of the knowledge of good and evil, for when you eat from it you will certainly die." (Genesis 2:15–17)

Now the serpent was more crafty than any of the wild animals the LORD God had made. He said to the woman, "Did God really say …" (Genesis 3:1)

How much trouble do we get into when we question what God has said! It's not wrong to question something we don't understand, but if we question whether to obey God, or whether God is right, or whether His Word is outdated, we're asking for trouble.

Back to Genesis. We know Adam and Eve ate the forbidden fruit and were kicked out of the garden. If they were going to decide what was right and wrong for themselves, they could no longer have access to the Tree of Life in the garden. But that is not all. Adam was told that the earth would produce thorns and thistles and he'd have to work hard to grow food. He would no longer have dominion over the earth; it would fight him every step of the way. Not only that, without the Tree of Life, they would die. No one had done that yet. Did they even understand what that meant? On the surface, it looks like this part did not come true because Adam and Eve lived a very long time—over nine hundred years!

But God is not a liar; they did die. You see, we are threefold beings; we have spirits given us when God breathed His life into Adam. We have souls—minds, wills, and emotions. And we have bodies. Their spirit is what died. Adam and Eve could no longer live in fellowship with God. God is Spirit, and He is life. A dead spirit cannot be in relationship with Him. Everyone since Adam has inherited a dead spirit. So now what? Was humankind doomed?

No! From the beginning of creation, God knew what would happen, and He "counted the cost." He loved us so much and was willing to pay the price to buy back His children. Jesus chose to die for us before we were even born. When we choose to follow Jesus, our dead spirits are born again and there is a holy exchange—Jesus takes all our sin and gives us His righteousness and His right standing with Father God. Although that would definitely be enough, there's more.

Remember, God had created the earth and given dominion over it to Adam and Eve. God gave away His dominion over earth. That doesn't mean God was diminished in any way or that He was not sovereign or almighty; it just meant that His plan was for Adam and Eve to rule the earth. But—and this is a huge but—Adam and Eve listened to the crafty serpent, Satan, and lost their dominion over the earth to him! He then gained the authority to cause death, destruction, and perversion on the earth, and he certainly has. Scripture says that all creation groans waiting for redemption. Adam and Eve did more than just eat a piece of fruit. They sold their birthright—their inheritance—to the devil for an apple!

While on earth, Jesus talked over and over about the kingdom of God and the kingdom of heaven. He told His disciples that "the kingdom of God is near" or "the kingdom of God is at hand." What does this mean?

The Jewish people thought this meant that they would be able to kick Rome out of Israel and have their nation back. But that is not what happened. Because of their ideas of what God was going to do, how, and when, they missed what God was doing right under their noses. They didn't understand, so Jesus told many parables trying to explain what the kingdom of heaven was like.

> Blessed are the poor in spirit, for theirs is the kingdom of heaven. (Matthew 5:3)

> For I tell you that unless your righteousness surpasses that of the Pharisees and the teachers of the law, you will certainly not enter the kingdom of heaven. (Matthew 5:20)

> Not everyone who says to me, "Lord, Lord," will enter the kingdom of heaven, but only the one who does the will of my Father who is in heaven. (Matthew 7:21)

In Matthew 13, Jesus said the kingdom of heaven was like

- a man who sowed good seed in his field. But while everyone was sleeping, his enemy came and sowed weeds among the wheat, and went away (v. 24)

- a mustard seed, which a man took and planted in his field. Though it is the smallest of all seeds, yet when it grows, it is the largest of garden plants and becomes a tree, so that the birds come and perch in its branches (vv. 31–32)

- yeast that a woman took and mixed into about sixty pounds of flour until it worked all through the dough (v. 33)

- treasure hidden in a field. When a man found it, he hid it again, and then in his joy went and sold all he had and bought that field. (v. 44)

- a merchant looking for fine pearls. When he found one of great value, he went away and sold everything he had and bought it. (vv. 45–46)

- a net that was let down into the lake and caught all kinds of fish. When it was full, the fishermen pulled it up on the shore. Then they sat down and collected the good fish in baskets, but threw the bad away. (v. 47)

Jesus told us to pray, "Thy kingdom come, thy will be

done, on earth as it is in heaven." If we are asking for God's kingdom to come, for His will to be done, we are letting go of our priorities and choosing His. We are asking Him to change our hearts to want what He wants. One translation reads, "thy kingdom come in earth as it is in heaven" (Matthew 6:10 KJV). We were made from the dust of the earth. The first place God's kingdom must come is in us. Jesus said in Luke 17:21 (KJV), "The kingdom of God is within you."

Is there strife in heaven? No. Is there sickness in heaven? No. Is there fear, selfishness, unforgiveness, pride, jealously, or criticism in heaven? Again, no. Those are easy answers. If it's not in heaven, His will is that it not be on earth either.

What about our more-complicated lives? What about those situations where we really don't know what to pray or what we really want to pray is not what Jesus would do?

When one of those sticky situations come up, I often meditate on it. Now, lest you think me super spiritual, let me tell you what kind of meditating I do. I chew on it. I imagine conversations, scenarios, solutions, consequences, and so on. I figure out exactly what will need to be done and said. Then I tell God how to fix the situation. In the past, I actually told God, "Lord, here's the situation. Now if you cannot figure

it out, just follow my step-by-step plan and it will work!"
Remembering that makes me laugh, but back then, I was
serious—way too serious. Now, years later, I'm not quite that
blatant, but I still tend to meditate too much. God doesn't
need my help figuring out what to do. He is not up in heaven
wringing His hands or pacing the streets of gold wondering
how He is going to handle the problem.

We can pray His kingdom, His will into that problem. *Father
Knows Best* is more than an old TV show—He really does!

Do you know someone whose life is in shambles? Is your
life in turmoil? Do you need guidance? Do you need provision
or help? You can call the kingdom of God—"Thy kingdom
come"—into your life, your situation. This is saying, "God,
I don't know what is best right here. And the enemy is really
working in this situation. But God, I want your will here.
You defeated Satan. He won't win! I don't know how you
are going to work this out, but it is in your hands. I give you
permission. You are Lord. You are right. You know exactly
what is needed here. You see the big picture. I take my hands
off. Your kingdom come, Your will be done—which is much
better than my will any day of the week. And Lord, if I'm
supposed to do something, please let me know. Guide me."

We could study the kingdom and never understand all there is to know about it. But I want to highlight two other scriptures here.

> The Law and the Prophets were proclaimed until John. Since that time, the good news of the kingdom of God is being preached, and everyone is forcing their way into it. (Luke 16:16)

John the Baptist was the end of an era, the last prophet of the Old Testament. Jesus started a new era, the restoration of the kingdom of God on earth. But it doesn't just happen. You cannot get there by accident. Imagine trying to cross a river with a strong current. You cannot just float across to the other side because the current will carry you downstream and eventually over the falls. It takes effort and determination to get to the other side. The same is true of the kingdom of heaven. We must intentionally follow Jesus; we must choose to act according to kingdom principles. It won't just happen no matter how much God wants it. He gives us a choice.

> I will give you the keys of the kingdom of
> heaven; whatever you bind on earth will be
> bound in heaven, and whatever you loose on
> earth will be loosed in heaven. (Matthew 16:19)

The kingdom of heaven is where God lives and reigns. He is love. He is life. There is no anger, jealously, unforgiveness, fear, negativity, sickness, deception, and so on in His kingdom. We have to learn a whole new way of talking. We must learn to speak truth. We must learn to forgive and so on. If we are carrying anything not of God's kingdom in our memories and emotions, we can choose to loose them from our soul with the authority that Jesus has given us. Then we can bind God's truths, His love, His peace, His acceptance to our soul. Such freedom!

As we seek God's kingdom, we will learn truths that open up doors of understanding, keys on how to pray, and so on. One of these keys is forgiveness. We'll talk more about that later. Another key is speaking truth. What God has said is true, whether we see it, or understand it, or even like it. We should speak more about God's goodness, faithfulness, and promises than about the problems.

Discussion Questions

Read Matthew 13:1–23 (NLT) about the sower sowing seed.

> Later that same day Jesus left the house and sat beside the lake. A large crowd soon gathered around him, so he got into a boat. Then he sat there and taught as the people stood on the shore. He told many stories in the form of parables, such as this one:
>
> "Listen! A farmer went out to plant some seeds. As he scattered them across his field, some seeds fell on a footpath, and the birds came and ate them. Other seeds fell on shallow soil with underlying rock. The seeds sprouted quickly because the soil was shallow. But the plants soon wilted under the hot sun, and since they didn't have deep roots, they died. Other seeds fell among thorns that grew up and choked out the tender plants. Still other seeds fell on fertile soil, and they produced a crop that was thirty, sixty, and even a hundred times as much as had

been planted! Anyone with ears to hear should listen and understand.

"Now listen to the explanation of the parable about the farmer planting seeds: The seed that fell on the footpath represents those who hear the message about the Kingdom and don't understand it. Then the evil one comes and snatches away the seed that was planted in their hearts. The seed on the rocky soil represents those who hear the message and immediately receive it with joy. But since they don't have deep roots, they don't last long. They fall away as soon as they have problems or are persecuted for believing God's word. The seed that fell among the thorns represents those who hear God's word, but all too quickly the message is crowded out by the worries of this life and the lure of wealth, so no fruit is produced. The seed that fell on good soil represents those who truly hear and understand God's word and produce a harvest of thirty, sixty, or even a hundred times as much as had been planted!"

Think about the different places the seed lands. What kind of ground have you been at different times in your life? Can you choose what kind of ground you want to be? (Yes.)

What kinds of fruit might be produced during those seasons?

What are some ways we can be "intentional" about the kingdom of God?

Prayer

Father,

I pray, "Thy Kingdom come, Thy will be done" first in me. Please change me from the inside out. Change my likes and desires and attitudes. Just like children resemble their earthly parents, let others see you in me. Let them hear you and your love come out of my mouth. I can't make that happen by myself.

Holy Spirit, you live in me. Please clean me from the inside out. Fill me with your light, joy, and peace. Make me so full of you and your Living Water that I splash your kingdom on all those around me.

God, you are the master gardener. Please soften the hard paths in my life. Remove the weeds and thorns. Please make my heart fertile soil so your Word can produce fruit in my life.

And Father, for those I love who need you and your loving touch, let your kingdom come into their lives too. Let what is not of you make them so uncomfortable that they can't wait to let it go. Orchestrate circumstances and acquaintances to lead them to you. For those who know you, help them to know you more, to draw closer to you, and to hear your voice. Thank you for loving all of them with your everlasting love, which is so much greater than mine.

And for our country, thy kingdom come! Teach us to praise you for our blessings and not take them for granted and not take the credit ourselves. Raise up godly leaders. Show us how to be responsible citizens as we obey you first.

Thank you.

Give Us This Day Our Daily Bread

At first glance, this seems like such a simple prayer. "Lord, we need bread today." When I was a new believer learning about trusting God to take care of me, I really believed He would provide ... just barely. I could trust Him to provide me literally bread and water and a tent to live in—the bare necessities. I lived in Ohio at the time and could imagine living in a tent in the winter with frozen bread and ice cubes to live on. Can I say again, the bare necessities?

Little by little, as I grew closer to God, I found out He is a loving Father, and He wanted to take good care of me. So let's delve a little deeper into what Jesus taught us about praying for our needs.

Give. Why would He tell us to ask His Father for bread if God couldn't provide it or didn't want to? God is all sufficient; He is—and has—enough for us and everyone else. Jesus didn't say that we should beg God for bread; that would imply He didn't want to provide for us or wanted to see us grovel, to humiliate us. No! He wants to provide. He wants us to know we can rely on Him. He wants us to be His children, sons and daughters of the King, not beggars.

Jesus also did not say that God should pay us our daily bread. We buy bread with the pay we get for working, but we're not asking God to pay us according to our performance, according to what we deserve, according to the work we have done. We cannot earn His blessings or provision; they are His gifts to us, so we respond with thanksgiving. We must always be more interested in the giver than the gifts.

This day. God wants to provide today what we need today; it doesn't help us to get today's bread tomorrow or next week. God is never late. And He is never early either. His provision is always on time, not necessarily on our time but always at the right time.

Daily Bread. Every day, we have needs. And every day, our heavenly Father wants us to come to Him with our needs, wants, hopes, disappointments, and especially our hearts. He wants to enjoy our fellowship every day, not just when we need something, not just when we have a problem, not just on Sunday—every day. He loves spending time with us.

Now let's look at this from another viewpoint. Jesus said to pray, "Give us this day our daily bread." He also told Satan when He was being tempted, "Man shall not live by bread alone, but on every word that comes from the mouth of God" (Matthew 4:4). In another place, He said, "I am the Bread of Life" (John 6:35). When Jesus told us to pray for our daily bread, He was talking more than whole wheat or pumpernickel; He is our daily bread. He wants our whole being to be healthy and well fed, not just our bodies.

When you spend time in His Word and talking to Him, your spirit and soul are nourished too, so you need to feed on His Word daily. Ask the Holy Spirit to sink His truth deep into your inner being to heal you, to show you where you've believed lies, and to replace those lies with His truth to cleanse your soul (mind, will, and emotions). This is renewing your mind. Learn to think God's thoughts. Sometimes, you might read a chapter or two. Sometimes, one verse will jump off the page and you'll meditate on it for days. Choose to feed your spirit, not just your body.

Another time, He told His disciples, "My food, said Jesus,

is to do the will of him who sent me [His Father] and to finish his work" (John 4:34). We are the hands and feet of Jesus here on earth. He has assignments for each of us. Ephesians 2:10 (NLT) tells us, "For we are God's masterpiece. He has created us anew in Christ Jesus, so we can do the good things he planned for us long ago."

We are told in John 3:16, "God so loved the world that he gave his one and only Son." Does the world know this? Nope, it really doesn't. God has reached out to us through someone, and He has someone for us to reach out to with His love. I am surprised when I hear of people in the United States coming to Christ at age thirty or forty never having heard from anyone that God loved them and had sent Jesus for their salvation.

Ask the Holy Spirit to lead you. You don't need to walk around with a ten-pound Bible preaching on the street corner; you yourself are the only Bible some people will ever read. Let God love people through what you do and say. Ask for His guidance daily.

Are you uncomfortable asking God for your needs? Many people won't pray for themselves believing it's self-centered to do so and that they should only pray for others. We should pray for ourselves and others—both!

What about needs that aren't daily bread needs such as guidance, a new job, relationship issues, and so on? Shortly after Jesus taught the disciples to pray, He said,

> So I say to you: Ask and it will be given to you; seek and you will find; knock and the door will be opened to you. For everyone who asks receives; the one who seeks finds; and to the one who knocks, the door will be opened. (Luke 11:9–10)

The words translated ask, seek, and knock here actually mean, "Ask, and keep on asking. Seek, and keep on seeking. Knock, and keep on knocking." God is our heavenly Father, not a vending machine. Sometimes, we get frustrated when we don't see answers to our prayers right away. As we ask and keep on asking, sometimes, our prayers change. Maybe we've been asking for the wrong thing. Many times, I've been glad God didn't answer my prayer the way I originally prayed it. Maybe our motives are not quite right. Maybe the timing isn't quite right. Remember, we are praying for His kingdom to come. God answers all prayers, but sometimes, the answers are no or not now. If we are praying according to something He has promised, His answer will always be yes!

After teaching about asking, seeking and knocking, Jesus asked,

> Which of you fathers, if your son asks for a fish, will give him a snake instead? Or if he asks for an egg, will give him a scorpion? If you then, though you are evil, know how to give good gifts to your children, how much more will your Father in heaven give the Holy Spirit to those who ask him! (Luke 11:11–13)

Two things here: first, trust that your heavenly Father loves you. He is good, and He has only good gifts for you. He won't give you something that will harm you. Second, He is telling you to ask for the Holy Spirit, so you should indeed ask! This is something you can pray for over and over.

As we grow in the Lord and get rid of our junk, we can contain more of the Holy Spirit. We don't actually get more in quantity, but He gets more of us!

Discussion Questions

Do you have trouble trusting God to take care of you? Just barely? Like a much-loved child?

Do you have trouble understanding the Bible? What version do you use?

Do you feed your inner man as well as you feed your outer man?

When was the last time you told someone that God really loved him or her?

Whom do you know who really needs to know about Jesus and what He has done for him or her?

Have you ever prayed for something and you were glad God didn't give it to you?

Do you pray to be filled and refilled with the Holy Spirit? Remember, sometimes we leak!

Prayer

Father God,

Thank you for wanting to be more than just my God but also wanting to be my heavenly Father. No other religion has a God like you. Teach me deep inside what that means. Teach me that I can trust you and how to trust you in every area of my life. Teach me how to feed not just my body but also my inner self. Make me as hungry for more of you as I am for food. And Lord, guide me as I share your love with others. Lead me to those who desperately need you. Show me how to love with your love. Give me the right words to say to share your love even if that means no words for a while. Thank you, Holy Spirit, for your guidance and help today and every day.

And Lord, when I don't see answers right away, I will trust that you are answering in the best way for me. You may be getting me ready first.

You may be showing me that I need to adjust my prayer. You may be closing the wrong doors so the right door can open. I will trust you.

Holy Spirit, I need you, today, now, always!

I pray in Jesus's precious name, amen.

Forgive Us Our Sins

Forgive us our sins. Each word of this phrase is so full of meaning, so critical.

Forgive

As per Dictonary.com, to forgive is

- to grant pardon for or remission of (an offense, debt, etc.); absolve
- to give up all claim on account of; remit (a debt, obligation, etc.)
- to grant pardon to (a person)
- to cease to feel resentment against: to forgive one's enemies
- to cancel an indebtedness or liability of: to forgive the interest owed on a loan

To forgive means letting go of whatever is owed, to cancel a debt.

Us and Our

I think Jesus put this part before forgiving others for a good reason. It is much easier to deal with how people have sinned against us after we first look at our sins. It helps us to approach others with humility and compassion instead of self-righteous arrogance.

Sins

What exactly are sins? Some of the definitions in *Merriam-Webster's* are these.

- an offense against religious or moral law
- a transgression of the law of God

Some time ago, I attended a rehearsal for my sister's wedding, which was to take place in a Catholic church. After the rehearsal, the priest announced that he would hear the confession of anyone interested. I had been raised a Catholic, but at the time, I was a new believer who hadn't yet switched churches, so I went to confession. However, I wasn't sure what to confess, so I ran through the Ten Commandments: I wasn't praying to any other gods. I didn't swear using God's name. I went to church on Sunday, and I didn't have to obey my parents anymore. I hadn't killed anyone—and so on. The priest asked me, "What about sins against the law of love?" Ouch! He had me there. I had a very narrow idea of what constituted sin.

Basically, sin is something done wrong. If we don't want to sin, we try to control what we do or don't do. That seems difficult enough, but maybe attainable … someday. But to make matters worse, the *Baltimore Catechism* (Catholic) defines sin as "any thought, word or deed that violates the laws of God." The *Westminster Shorter Catechism* explains it this way. "Sin is any want of conformity unto, or transgression of, the law of God." Those cover a lot of ground. We can understand that our words can be sinful—lies, gossip, or even just hurtful words. But can our thoughts be sinful? Let's look at what Jesus said in Matthew 5:21–22, 27–28.

> You have heard that it was said to the people long ago, "You shall not murder, and anyone who murders will be subject to judgment." But I

tell you that anyone who is angry with a brother or sister will be subject to judgment. Again, anyone who says to a brother or sister, "Raca," [an Aramaic term of contempt] is answerable to the court. And anyone who says, "You fool!" will be in danger of the fire of hell. (This makes me watch my mouth while driving in traffic.)

You have heard that it was said, "You shall not commit adultery." But I tell you that anyone who looks at a woman lustfully has already committed adultery with her in his heart.

In Matthew 12:36–37 Jesus said,

But I tell you that men will have to give account on the Day of Judgment for every careless word they have spoken. For by your words you will be acquitted, and by your words you will be condemned.

Just looking at these few verses should be enough to convince us that we have all sinned. We must agree with

Romans 3:10: "As it is written: 'There is no one righteous, not even one.'" We all need forgiveness from God.

Through Jesus's death on the cross, He forgave all our sins. No sin no matter how horrible is stronger than His blood, and I'm so thankful for that. All our sinful thoughts, words, and actions are not just hidden, but gone—cleansed. Psalm 103:12 (NLT) tells us, "He has removed our sins as far from us as the east is from the west." Notice that he didn't write as far as the north is from the south. If you go far enough north, you will reach the North Pole; keep going, and you'll eventually get to the South Pole. But as far as the east is from the west, east never reaches west.

When God created Adam and Eve and put them in the Garden of Eden, everything was perfect. They had everything they needed and close fellowship with God as well. They knew Him, and they knew that He was good and that He loved them. God had given them over two thousand kinds of fruit to eat, but they wanted more. They decided God was holding out on them.

God had told Adam and Eve that if they ate from the Tree of Knowledge of Good and Evil, they would die. But they lived a long time; Adam lived over nine hundred years! So was God wrong? Did He lie? Was it an idle threat? Nope!

To better understand this, we have to realize that we are threefold beings—we are spirits (the part of us that can have a relationship with a spirit God) souls (mind, will and emotions), and bodies. Adam's and Eve's bodies didn't die; their spirits did. They were no longer in God's kingdom and were thus subject to sin, Satan, and death.

And if that weren't bad enough, they now had dead spirits ruled by sin, and they passed that sinful, fallen nature on to all their descendants, including us. Adam and Eve could no longer have an intimate relationship with God, and neither can we—without Jesus. That is why we must be born again. Our spirits must be born again, given life. But how? Listen to what the Word of God says.

> Jesus answered and said to him, "Truly, truly, I say to you, unless one is born again, he cannot see the kingdom of God." (John 3:3 ESV)

> That which is born of the flesh is flesh, and that which is born of the Spirit is spirit. (John 3:6 ESV)

Praise be to the God and Father of our Lord Jesus Christ! In his great mercy he has given us new birth into a living hope through the resurrection of Jesus Christ from the dead. (1 Peter 1:3)

For you have been born again, not of perishable seed, but of imperishable, through the living and enduring word of God. (1 Peter 1:23)

Jesus Christ, through the Holy Spirit, comes to live in us and makes us new creations. Our sinful nature is dead. God isn't trying to fix our old man; it was too far gone. He killed it. Our sins were forgiven by the shed blood of Jesus, and our old, sinful natures were crucified with Christ on that cross.

My old self has been crucified with Christ. It is no longer I who live, but Christ lives in me. So, I live in this earthly body by trusting in the Son of God, who loved me and gave himself for me. (Galatians 2:20 NLT)

This means that anyone who belongs to Christ has become a new person. The old life is gone;

a new life has begun! (2 Corinthians 5:17 NLT; the NIV version says, "Therefore, if anyone is in Christ, the new creation has come. The old has gone, the new is here!")

But what about now, after salvation, after Jesus cleansed us from sin? Are we immediately perfect? No, we still sin! We still want our own way. We forget or ignore the fact that our Father knows best and we rebel. What do we do? Do we just throw up our hands in desperation and give up? Or worse, just excuse ourselves by saying, "Everyone does it!" or "No one is perfect!"? Or do we just try harder? Paul wrote in Romans 7:15–26 (NLT),

I don't really understand myself, for I want to do what is right, but I don't do it. Instead, I do what I hate. But if I know that what I am doing is wrong, this shows that I agree that the law is good. So, I am not the one doing wrong; it is sin living in me that does it.

And I know that nothing good lives in me, that is, in my sinful nature. I want to do what is right, but I can't. I want to do what is good, but I don't. I don't want to do what is wrong, but I do it anyway. But if I do what I don't want to do, I am not really the one doing wrong; it is sin living in me that does it.

I have discovered this principle of life—that when I want to do what is right, I inevitably do what is wrong. I love God's law with all my heart. But there is another power within me that is at war with my mind. This power makes me a slave to the sin that is still within me. Oh, what a miserable person I am! Who will free me from this life that is dominated by sin and death? Thank God! The answer is in Jesus Christ our Lord. So, you see how it is: In my mind I really want to obey God's law, but because of my sinful nature I am a slave to sin.

Can you identify with Paul in this? I know I can! Is it hopeless? Yes—without Jesus.

So what do we do when we sin now? Jesus cancelled our debt. He paid the price with His blood. He has forgiven us our sins—things we've done and things we didn't do but should have. And He has thrown our sins into the sea of forgetfulness. What has been forgiven is gone. God has chosen to forget, and He will never throw it back in our face. Satan will, but God won't!

Once we have admitted that we need Jesus's forgiveness and received Him into our hearts as our Savior, we are forgiven. Completely. All our sins are washed away—past, present, and future—and our old, dead spirit man was nailed to the cross with Jesus. Our spirit is instantly reborn.

But you say, "I keep sinning!" Yes, we all still have sin habits. That doesn't change whether we are forgiven or not. Hebrews 7:25 tells us, "Therefore he is able to save completely those who come to God through him, because he always lives to intercede for them." Completely! Let that sink in.

When we fail, we confess our sins to God but not to be forgiven because we are already forgiven; we confess, acknowledge, that what we did was wrong, that we fell short of the glory of God, and we ask for help. We need to learn to act according to the kingdom of God. We need to learn to love with His love, speak words full of His truth, and walk as He walked. That is the ongoing Christian walk. Choosing to be a Christ follower is not a one-time event but an ongoing, daily choice. That's why God sent His Holy Spirit to be our helper, and we all need His help!

Remember that we are threefold beings—spirits, souls, and bodies. When we are born again, our spirits are instantly reborn, but our souls and bodies are not. If we have pimples when we receive Jesus, most likely they'll still be there in the morning. If we have been rejected, abandoned, or betrayed, those hurts won't go away immediately. Our minds need to be renewed by being cleansed when we read and meditate on His Word and spend time in worship and prayer. Our souls, emotions, and wills need to be healed. Everyone has wounds; some are more visible than others. If we are wounded in our emotions and full of shame, we are prone to believe lies like these.

- I'm unlovable.
- I'm unworthy.
- I'll never amount to anything.
- I can't do anything right.
- I've been used and abused and no one will ever want me.
- I'm unwanted.
- I'm a mistake.

These are healed by the Word of God, His healing love, and His people. This takes time. We are all works in progress.

Discussion Questions

Have you received Jesus's forgiveness for your sins?

Do you keep asking forgiveness for the same things over and over?

Do you have trouble believing you are forgiven?

Do you ask for the Holy Spirit's help daily?

Prayer

Precious Jesus,

Thank you for taking the punishment for my sins. You didn't deserve to die. I did. But you chose to take all God's anger, which I deserved, onto yourself on the cross. My debt has been cancelled. Paid in full. I choose to follow you today and forever. I know you will never leave me or give up on me, and you always keep your promises.

Thank you that I am a new creation. My spirit can now have a close, intimate relationship with you. You said I could come right into your courts, your throne room, with thanksgiving and praise. You live in me and are changing me from the inside out. Help me to walk and talk every day like your child.

Thank you that I am yours and that there is now no condemnation because I am in Christ Jesus. Lord, your Word says you see me and know me. I thank you for having good plans for me and for working out everything, even my past, for my good as I follow and serve you. You are amazing, God, and I love you.

In Jesus's precious name, amen.

As We Forgive Those Who Sin against Us

Forgive us as we forgive others—that's certainly a new twist on the golden rule: do unto others as you would have them do unto you. We are talking to God here. Do we really want Him to forgive us the way we forgive those who mess with us?

Most people acknowledge that they have sinned and need God's forgiveness. Those who don't admit they need forgiveness often think that good intentions or even ignorance makes everything okay, but God's Word doesn't support that line of thought. According to Romans 3:23, "all have sinned." That word *all* there is the Greek word *pas*, and really means all—you, me, and everyone else. So we all definitely need God's forgiveness. But in the same measure we forgive others? That's a scary thought. We definitely need to explore this a bit further.

Let's look at the parable of the unmerciful servant.

Then Peter came to Jesus and asked, "Lord, how many times shall I forgive my brother or sister who sins against me? Up to seven times?" Jesus answered, "I tell you, not seven times, but seventy-seven times." [Some translations say seventy times seven—a lot.] Therefore, the kingdom of heaven is like a king who wanted to settle accounts with his servants. As he began the settlement, a man who owed him ten thousand bags of gold was brought to him. Since he was not able to pay, the master ordered that he and his wife and his children and all that he had be sold to repay the debt.

"At this the servant fell on his knees before him. 'Be patient with me,' he begged, 'and I will pay back everything.' The servant's master took pity on him, canceled the debt and let him go.

"But when that servant went out, he found one of his fellow servants who owed him a hundred silver coins. He grabbed him and began to choke him. 'Pay back what you owe me!' he demanded.

"His fellow servant fell to his knees and begged him, 'Be patient with me, and I will pay it back.'

"But he refused. Instead, he went off and had the man thrown into prison until he could pay the debt. When the other servants saw what had happened, they were outraged and went and told their master everything that had happened.

"Then the master called the servant in. 'You wicked servant,' he said, 'I canceled all that debt of yours because you begged me to. Shouldn't you have had mercy on your fellow servant just as I had on you?' In anger his master handed him over to the jailers to be tortured, until he should pay back all he owed.

"This is how my heavenly Father will treat each of you unless you forgive your brother or sister from your heart."

Notice a couple things in this story. First of all, the master was owed a debt. How he had run up that much of a tab is beyond me. He must have kept giving and giving even when the servant was not able to pay back. Sounds like God. He gives and gives, more than we deserve.

Second, the servant had received much and he owed a huge debt, one he could never repay. Never, as in more than one lifetime. No hope! By law, the servant and his whole family could have been sold into slavery to pay the debt or put in debtors' prison. But even that would not have completely paid the debt.

Third, the master forgave this enormous debt. He wanted to settle accounts. He didn't want the debt to come between them. God doesn't want our debt to come between Him and us. He wants relationship! So the master took the debt upon himself. In essence, he paid it. Jesus paid our debt—one we owed but could not repay; one He didn't owe but paid anyway.

Do you think the servant was grateful? Maybe, but not grateful enough. He had a debtor who owed him not a huge amount but more than he could repay immediately. Did he have mercy on his fellow servant? Nope! He "had the man thrown into prison until he could pay the debt." That is what the master could have done to him. Unbelievable! Couldn't he see what he was doing? Others did, and they were angry. They told the master, who reacted the same way. He must have asked himself, *How could my servant do that? Did he not understand how much he had been forgiven? Did he somehow think he deserved forgiveness and the other man did not?*

He called the servant to appear before him. The debt the master had forgiven was now unforgiven! "In anger his master handed him over to the jailers to be tortured, until he should pay back all he owed," which would be never. That is heavy. It sure tells us that forgiveness is important. But exactly what is it, and how do we do it?

Jesus taught His disciples to pray. Matthew 6:12 says, "And forgive us our debts, as we also have forgiven or debtors." The same passage in Luke 11 says, "Forgive us our sins, for we also forgive anyone who sins against us." When someone hurts us deliberately or not, what do we feel he or she owes us? An apology? Repayment? Acknowledgment that he or she was wrong? Restoration of what was lost if that's even possible? Understanding? Somehow, they should have to suffer the same way you have! That sounds a lot like revenge.

In Romans 12:17 (NLT), Paul quoted Deuteronomy 32:35.

> Dear friends, never take revenge. Leave that to the righteous anger of God. For the Scriptures say, "'I will take revenge; I will pay them back,' says the LORD."

Forgiveness lets go of whatever we are owed. It cancels the debt. An apology might be nice and even deserved, but we will not demand that, or punish a debtor, or expect restitution. The Lord has promised to restore the years the locust has eaten so He can more than make up for our loss (Joel 2:25).

I want to touch on a few more aspects of forgiveness. First, we need forgiveness from God. Adam and Eve sinned and passed on their sinful, fallen nature to us, and we do more than our fair share of sinning. But as I mentioned, Jesus paid the price with His blood for our sins, and what has been forgiven is gone.

Second, people sin against one another. We've all been hurt by what others have done or not done to us, and it can be very hard to forgive them. And forgiving ourselves is even harder, but it's just as important. God knew how we would mess up before we were even born. He's got it covered. Give it to Him, and He can turn even our messes into messages, our failures into testimonies. Satan hates testimonies because they give others hope and encouragement that God can save and rescue them too, that nothing is too big for God, and that no one is too far down in the pit for God to reach him or her.

This subject would not be complete unless we mention forgiving God. That's right; we often need to forgive Him. Not that He has done anything wrong, but we sometimes get mad at Him. I know that seems almost too outrageous to say, but it boils down to our not believing that He is good, that He loves us, and that He is much smarter than we are. But if we are mad at Him maybe from way before we knew Him, we should tell Him. He's a big God; He can handle it. He knows anyway. Give Him the hurt, the disappointment, even the pride that you thought you were "gooder" than Him. He's holding you now just as He was holding you then.

Let's talk a minute about what forgiveness is not. Forgiving someone is not saying that whatever that person did that hurt us was right or good. Forgiveness does not excuse bad behavior. Forgiveness does not mean trust is restored and a relationship is automatically restored to what it was before.

(It might open the door to a restored relationship, but it's not automatic.) Forgiveness does not mean that all the hurt goes away immediately or that you forget the wrong and the hurt. God is able to forgive and forget. It does mean that we no longer bring up the incident every time the topic arises. When we choose to forgive, we acknowledge that we have been forgiven and released from what we deserve, and we will obey God and release others.

A Few Practical Notes

Forgiveness is a process, especially if our wounds are deep or ongoing. If the wound is deep like rejection, humiliation, betrayal, abandonment, and so on, forgiveness is a choice, an act of our will, and many times, we release over and over. I have often revisited the same event several times and forgiven a hurt from a slightly different perspective each time. However, the hurts heal at different rates. Reading scripture and letting the truth of God's Word settle in our hearts helps.

If you have been betrayed, remember that Jesus understands betrayal. He was betrayed by a good friend who had walked closely with Him for three years. If you have been rejected, Jesus understands that too; He was rejected. His own brothers didn't believe in Him. They thought He was crazy. People who hailed Him one day were calling for His crucifixion a few days later. And people are still rejecting Him every day. At one time or another, we have rejected Him.

Some of God's promises that have been especially comforting to me are these.

- Hebrews 13:5 (ESV): "I will never leave you nor forsake you." (To me, that said He'd never abandon me, nor throw up His hands in disgust and give up on me.)
- Psalm 27:10 (NLT): "Even if my father and mother abandon me, the LORD will hold me close."
- Psalm 139:5: "You hem me in behind and before, and you lay your hand upon me." (That always made me feel trapped until I found out it was the same word used in Psalm 34:7, which says, "The angel of the LORD encamps around those who fear him, and he delivers them." He hems me in with protection!)
- 1 John 1:9: "If we confess our sins, he is faithful and just and will forgive us our sins and purify us from all unrighteousness." (He forgives me and is purifying me.)

About Ongoing Hurts

Forgiveness is essential. So is wisdom. If you are in a relationship or situation in which you are continually being attacked, rejected, or hurt, give yourself some space. Seek counsel. Staying in a toxic relationship doesn't make you holy or more loving; it makes you wounded. Sometimes, you even need to leave whether temporarily or permanently. Jesus was betrayed and rejected, and they tried to kill Him twice, but He never let others have their way with Him until it was time for our redemption. No one took His life. He laid it down in God's timing.

Discussion Questions

Do you feel that God has been holding out on you? Could He do a better job taking care of you?

Do you have anyone you have had difficulty forgiving? Anyone you need to forgive repeatedly?

Do you have broken relationships? Are you praying for them to be restored? Or were they toxic and needed to end?

Do you need to ask Father God to heal your wounded heart?

Do you ask for the Holy Spirit's help daily?

Prayer

> Precious Jesus, thank you for taking the punishment for my sins. You didn't deserve to die—I did. But you chose to take all God's anger that I deserved onto yourself on the cross. You paid my debt in full. I choose to follow you today and forever. I know you will never leave me or give up on me, and you always keep your promises.
>
> Lord, you know who has hurt me or lied to me or about me, rejected me, betrayed me, or abandoned me. I know those hurts weren't your idea; they were theirs. Thank you for holding me through all those times even if I didn't know you were there. I choose to forgive them and release them and the hurts to you. Please heal

those hurts deep in me. Let your truth replace the lies I've believed.

Come, Holy Spirit. Fill me. Strengthen me. Enable me to walk as your child according to your kingdom.

In Jesus's precious name, amen.

And Lead Us Not into Temptation, But Deliver Us from Evil

When Jesus taught His disciples this pattern to pray, He started by pointing them to their heavenly Father. I believe that is important to remember at all times but especially during "lead me" and "deliver me" prayers.

We all know that not everyone is safe to follow and that not all deliverers really have the power and wisdom to deliver what they promise. But our heavenly Father sees the whole picture. He knows us inside and out, and He sees down the road to where we are going. He can be trusted to lead and deliver.

I never thought much about this line from the Lord's Prayer; I thought of it as the beginning of the end, part of the amen. And I really didn't understand it. If Jesus was telling us to ask Father God *not* to lead us into temptation, did that mean that God *wanted* to lead us there? That didn't sit right because God is a good Father. So I began digging and reading.

The word *tempt* means to "entice or attempt to entice (someone) to do ... or acquire something ... that they find attractive but know to be wrong or not beneficial." The apostle James tells us in chapter 1, verse 13, "When tempted, no one should say, 'God is tempting me' for God cannot be tempted by evil, nor does he tempt anyone." That verse clarifies that God never tempts us. But what did Jesus mean when He told us to pray, "and lead us not into temptation"?

The more I thought and prayed about this, the more I believed I was reading the phrase incorrectly. I had been putting the word *not* in the wrong place. I'd been reading, "Lead us *not* ... into temptation" when I should have been reading, "Lead us ... *not* into temptation." Do you see the difference? The first reading sounds like God *would* lead us into temptation and we're asking Him not to lead us there. The second is asking God to lead us *away* from temptation, away from places, situations, and people that tempt us to sin.

If I need to lose weight, I can pray that God will lead me away from the bakery or those all-you-can-eat buffets. If I have trouble staying sexually pure, I can pray that God will lead me away from suggestive movies, books, and too much alone time with the opposite sex. If I have a problem with complaining, God can lead me to walk in gratitude. When we ask God to lead us from temptations and especially those we don't even know about, He will. Sometimes, these are people who will pull us down or away from Him.

The second thing I found is the word translated "tempt" is also rendered as "test" or "trial." God will not lead us into temptations, but He will most definitely lead us into trials and tests. He does that not to show us how weak we are but to teach and train us. He may show us where we need to grow or that we are growing and trusting Him more than the last time, that we're making progress.

What else does scripture tell us about being tempted? Matthew 3:13–17 records the baptism of Jesus by John the Baptist.

> Then Jesus came from Galilee to the Jordan to be baptized by John. But John tried to deter him, saying, "I need to be baptized by you, and do you come to me?" Jesus replied, "Let it be so now; it is proper for us to do this to fulfill all

righteousness." Then John consented. As soon as Jesus was baptized, he went up out of the water.

At that moment heaven was opened, and he saw the Spirit of God descending like a dove and alighting on him. And a voice from heaven said, *"This is my Son, whom I love; with him I am well pleased."* (emphasis mine)

Please note that Father God clearly says, "This is my Son, whom I love; with him I am well pleased." So what happens immediately afterward? Matthew 4:1 follows: "Then Jesus was led by the Spirit into the wilderness to be tempted by the devil." Does that sound like what a loving father would do? God had just said how pleased He was with Jesus and how much He loved Jesus.

Here again, the word *tempted* is better understood as tested. Jesus will encounter some trials designed to teach and equip Him for His purpose. Did you ever think about Jesus, the Son of God, needing to learn anything? Remember, He is fully God and fully man. He laid aside the perks of heaven to come down here and live as we do.

Hebrews 5:8 tells us that Jesus, Son though he was, learned obedience from what he suffered. Jesus, totally loved by Father God, was led by the Spirit into the wilderness, fasted for forty days, and was tempted by Satan. The correct word here is *tempted* ... Satan is the tempter! God tests. Satan tempts. Jesus met Satan head-on and was victorious. Satan threw scripture at Jesus trying to entice Him when He was weak from hunger to deny or shortcut His purpose on earth, but Jesus didn't fall for his tricks; He knew the scriptures too and knew His Father was good as were His purposes, so Satan couldn't trick Him.

This is where the "deliver us from evil" part comes into focus. When Jesus was led into the wilderness to be tempted, God knew that the enemy would be there. In the same way, when we go through tests and trials, the enemy of our souls— the one who wants us to fail, who wants to destroy us—will be there.

Jesus was prepared for this battle; He knew His Father, and He knew His Word. People training to recognize counterfeit money study the real thing first. As we spend time in prayer and read the truth of scripture, we learn to really know God and what He is like. We can then recognize the enemy.

When the devil whispers in our ears, "Where's God now? You're never going to make it! You're worthless! God lied to you! You're a failure!" and so on, it sounds like our own voices rattling around in our heads, but it's not. We need to recognize those thoughts and who is really doing the talking. They are the enemy's propaganda.

We need to focus for a minute on God's purposes for us. Did He want just servants? No. He already had the angels. God created us in His image, and He wants us as His children. But after the fall of Adam and Eve, everything changed. Yes, we are still triune beings—spirits, souls, and bodies—but with dead spirits until we're born again by the Holy Spirit.

God's goal is for us to become like Jesus. Does that seem impossible? It is in our own strength. There is absolutely no way we can pray enough, do enough, learn enough, or suffer enough to be more like Jesus. Is it thus hopeless? No! We are told in Philippians 2:13 that He is working in us, "for it is God who works in you to will and to act in order to fulfill his good purpose."

Our spirits, once born again, must grow up. Ephesians 4:11–15 tells us,

So Christ himself gave the apostles, the prophets, the evangelists, the pastors and teachers, to equip his people for works of service, so that the body of Christ may be built up until we all reach unity in the faith and in the knowledge of the Son of God and become mature, attaining to the whole measure of the fullness of Christ. Then we will no longer be infants, tossed back and forth by the waves, and blown here and there by every wind of teaching and by the cunning and craftiness of people in their deceitful scheming. Instead, speaking the truth in love, we will grow to become in every respect the mature body of him who is the head, that is, Christ.

Jesus is growing His church. He is the head, and we are His body.

When I think of tests and trials, I think of children learning to walk. We watch our little ones pulling up on furniture and falling on their bottoms. Then they try again and plop down again. They may even throw temper tantrums! Finally, they pull themselves up, stay up, take a step, and down they go. But ultimately, they're tottering between Mommy and

Daddy and learning to get around obstacles and finally even running ... everywhere. They've gone through their tests and trials successfully.

That's a very simplistic picture of our growing into Christ. Father God knows His purpose for our lives. He knows where He is leading us and what we need to be capable of when we get there. What lessons will we need to learn? What strengths will we need to develop? The Bible is full of examples of God using trials or life lessons to prepare His people to fulfill their purpose. If David hadn't learned to be a shepherd and fight off lions and bears and then lead a small army of men while running for his life, would he have been ready to lead the nation of Israel? If Joseph, the youngest son who was left to care for the sheep, hadn't been sold into slavery by his brothers, hadn't learned to be a good steward in his master's household, and hadn't been in prison so he could interpret dreams for the baker and cupbearer of Pharaoh, would he have been in position to save the nation of Egypt and his father's whole family? No. We have a really great promise in Romans 8:28–29.

And we know that in all things *God works for the good of those who love him,* who have been called according to his purpose. For those God foreknew he also predestined *to be conformed to the image of his Son,* that he might be the firstborn among many brothers and sisters. (emphasis mine)

Should this verse more accurately be translated "and lead us not into test and trials"? What did Jesus do? In the Garden of Gethsemane, Jesus knew He was about to face an intense trial. Was He looking forward to it? Humanly speaking, I don't think so because He prayed and asked His Father if there was any other way.

And then He said, "Yet not as I will, but as you will." (Matthew 26:39)

Here's my paraphrase: "Father, lead us away from temptations, and when we are tested, help us to remember that you are good, to recognize the enemy, and to use the sword of the Spirit, your Word."

Discussion Questions

Have you ever thought about Jesus's needing to learn anything before?

I've given some examples of God leading us away from temptation. Can you think of any others?

Can you remember a test that God led you through and what you learned?

What lies does the enemy tell you? What is the truth from God's Word about this?

Prayer

Father God,

I thank you so much for your unending love that you lavish on me, on us. Father, your ways are so much higher than mine, and you are good. Please lead me away from people, places, and thoughts that will harm me, and lead me closer to you and your people. Keep my feet on the right path and going where you want me to go.

And Father, help me discipline my mind to stay on track. When thoughts start racing through my mind, make me aware of their source. As I read your Word, sink your truths deep into my heart. Help me focus on you, your many blessings, and your truth about me, about you, and about those around me.

In Jesus's name, I ask these things, amen.

Yours, Mine, and Ours

Most of us grew up with at least the head knowledge that Jesus died for the sins of the world. And many of us—I hope all of us—became aware that meant He died for our sins too. It became very personal. Jesus was brutally whipped and then nailed to a cross, where He hung for hours suffering terribly for you, for me, and for everyone else. I've heard it said that the nails didn't hold Jesus on the cross, that love did.

I find it wonderfully healing and comforting to realize that God knew me before the earth was formed and chose me even though He knew me and all my faults. Ephesians 1:4 tells us, "For he chose us in him before the creation of the world to be holy and blameless in his sight."

But I have been realizing that Jesus taught us to pray to our Father, not my Father. I thought this was because His *our* referred to His and my Father. And that's true in part. But then He taught us to pray, "Forgive us our debts, as we forgive our debtors"; that couldn't possibly include Jesus because He never had any debts; He never sinned. I began to realize that Jesus taught us to pray corporately as well as personally; we are to pray and ask forgiveness for our families and our nation.

When I would start to pray "Our Father," I was uncomfortable though I wasn't sure why, but then the lights went on and I started to understand. My salvation in Jesus is personal, and I talk to my heavenly Father personally. He was *my* Father, and I didn't want to share him. I wanted to feel I could crawl up on His lap and not have to fight off the other kids! And picturing His lap big enough to hold everyone at the same time didn't help; I was lost in the crowd.

As I shared before, God's name El Shaddai means "many-breasted one," like a momma dog having enough places for each of her puppies to nurse. As I was one of twelve children, that was especially meaningful to me. I needed to know that Father God was enough for all of His children and especially me, and He is. He knows me individually. He knows the number of hairs on my head and on yours too. It is good and right to talk to Father God as my Father, but there's more.

After I began to understand that God is my Father, I

started to become more aware of how much He loves me, how He's held me and been with me even before I knew Him, how He teaches and leads me. I could relax in His love. I am learning to trust Him more and more.

So what is so important about praying "Our Father"? Father God loves all His children as much as He loves me. That may seem an obvious truth, and I knew it in my head, but I didn't know it in my heart. This is radically changing how I pray for others, for nations, for leaders, for people I don't like, for those in obvious sin, for everyone! I can pray that others come to know Him and His love and not call down judgment.

Many of us identify with the Prodigal Son, who willfully went his own way and did his own thing before coming to his senses in the pig pen and going back home to his father. I know I do. I can picture my Father waiting for me, longing for me to repent, turn around, and come home, and then throwing a party for me. That is so true.

But Father God is also still waiting! When God created Adam and Eve, He wanted children to love. Out of all creation, humankind alone is capable of relationship with Him. But that was lost when Adam and Eve sinned. So many people haven't yet turned around (that's what repent means) and come home. They are still lost, alone, and hungry, and He still longs for them. He still stands looking for them.

Because He is our Father, I can pray for others without judging them, still seeing the reality of how far they are from God as I was, but also knowing they are loved and Father God is wanting them to come home to Him, knowing He wants to restore them to His family.

So we pray, "Our Father, who art in heaven …"

Father God,

We read in Isaiah 9:6 that You are Everlasting Father, Mighty God, Prince of Peace, Wonderful Counselor.

I know You long for those lost to Your love.

Everlasting Father, Mighty God, Your heart is that no one should perish.

Holy Spirit, Wonderful Counselor,

> just like you hovered over the waters when the earth was empty and void,

>> hover over those who are empty and void without You.

Get their attention.

> Surround them in Your Light.

Speak truth to their hearts.

Separate the light from the darkness in

their hearts and minds.

Breathe on them, that they will wake up,

open their spiritual eyes

and come to know Jesus,

Who will wash them clean with His Blood shed for them,

set them free from all condemnation,

and fill them with His shalom peace,

for He is our Prince of Peace.

Printed in the United States
By Bookmasters